A Slice of Wales

'A collection of tales to tickle your taste buds'

Darn Bach o Gymru

'Casgliad o storïau gwerinol'

authors/awduron

Angela Gray, Hazel Thomas, Gareth Johns,
Anthony Evans, Geraldine Trotman
and Ana Rees

Published by
HAT Events

Please note: all food photographs are generic
examples and not of actual recipes, except for
Granddads chicken dumplings on page 52.

Food photography supplied courtesy of the Welsh Assembly Government

First Impression – 2009

ISBN 978-0-9562553-0-3

The authors gratefully acknowledge the support and assistance
of the Welsh Assembly Government, National Library of Wales,
Visit Wales, Pembrokeshire County Council, Carmarthenshire
County Council and The Welsh Whisky Company.

Printed in Wales at
Gomer Press, Llandysul, Ceredigion

Contents

Introduction

This book is truly A Slice of Wales, giving you a glimpse of how blessed we are with our food and culture and perhaps more importantly giving you the chance to recreate some wonderful recipes. Here in Wales we have always had good honest food, which often was the preserve of the country folk that raised the animals and grew the vegetables, but now everyone can get a True Taste of Wales. Since 2001 The True Taste Awards have recognised the excellence of our food producers. The message to our consumers is that our food is good food, with True Taste and a real pleasure to eat, summing up our thriving modern food industry.

I have had the honour of presenting the True Taste Awards since their inception, and every year have been amazed at the quality of the food and the innovation of our producers. I hope you enjoy A Slice of Wales, its recipes, and more importantly, meeting the authors face to face, and who knows perhaps you will be inspired to visit the Land of My Fathers.

Hywel James.

Hywel James was born and raised on a dairy farm in Pembrokeshire and has an intimate knowledge of the county and its people. He is an Honorary Citizen of Tennessee from his YFC (Young Farmers Club) exchange to the USA in 1978. He joined ITV Wales in the 1980's where he started a new agricultural series called Farming Wales which he worked on for 26 years. As well as his love of Rural Affairs, Hywel has played an important role in promoting and championing Welsh food. Hywel now works as a freelance broadcaster and journalist. hywel@hyweljames.com

"The True Taste awards were developed and launched as a response to the Agri-food Partnership requesting an awards scheme to recognise quality food and drink in Wales. The scheme is now managed by the Welsh Assembly Government. "

Angela Gray

I feel very fortunate and grateful for being able to earn a living doing what I love. It's quite ironic that I didn't even contemplate making a career in the food world. I wanted to be a makeup artist, go to Hollywood, meet Harrison Ford, and have his babies. Such dreams, conjured up by a young girl growing up on a farm on top of Caerphilly Mountain, were soon quashed by a sobering dose of reality.

I remember working in London at The Carlton Tower Hotel in Knightsbridge, a customer who knew I had a keen interest in food gave me an American Express calendar featuring great chefs and the recipes of their signature dishes. As I read through the ingredients of the Roux Brothers, Anton Mosimann, Anton Edelmann and Raymond Blanc, I felt as if I could taste their dishes. It was clear right there and then where my future was heading. I had always had an interest in food, in the 60's my mother collected a series of Cordon Bleu magazines. A little later I discovered Mrs. Beeton, Elizabeth David, Sally Clarke and Jane Grigson who helped me realise there was room for women in a male-dominated world. Dreams of Harrison faded, I fell in love with food, and I never looked back.

I admit I am not classically trained; my career is the result of an infectious passion for food, a continuous quest to learn more, a creative and experimental mind, and most importantly the beginning, which was my inherited food knowledge, from mother, father, grandmother, great grandmother, aunts and an amazing domestic science teacher, Miss Price. On reflection, these people helped shape my future; they helped me create the building blocks of what was to become a rich and fruitful career, with endless opportunities and surprises. I feel indebted to those people, and my involvement in Wales Smithsonian Cymru is for them, to honour them, and a public opportunity to say thanks.

My father was born in Corris, a small slate mining village in Mid Wales. His

Bridge Street Corris at a time when there was a Post Office,
Iron Mongers, Butcher, Cobbler, Newsagent, Pub and General Stores.

father Iorweth was one of fourteen children (not all survived), born to Ellen Lloyd, who by all accounts was quite a lady. In her later years she travelled from Corris to America to claim an inheritance, and whilst there she studied the writings of Abraham Lincoln. She returned with her inheritance and subsequently purchased many properties in Corris. One was 'Hyfrydle' where my dad was born, and another was the post office and general store that was eventually to become our family retreat.

I grew up eating a mix of dishes. My dad knew and had learnt to make traditional Welsh foods, whilst my mother had more of an international flair based on her interest in cookery, which unusually came from my grandfather, and not my grandmother, who despised the kitchen. In her defence she was a business lady, but still expected to take care of all domestic duties. A little ingenuity was employed to deliver the meals, she became the queen of convenience, serving up all manner of concoctions using tins, packets, frozen and dried food, and she was resourceful to a fault. This left enough time for running the business and a weekly trip to London for a hair creation, a new outfit and everything to match.

On the other hand my father's family cooked and baked every day. I can remember arriving at *Nain*'s (Welsh for grandmother) house in Pennal after a long journey, to be welcomed not only with open arms and hearts, but with the aromas and promise of a special supper. A bubbling stew or *cawl*, slow roasted lamb or steak and kidney pie and most definitely a steamed pudding or fruit crumble. There would be a just cooked plate of Welshcakes on the table, a fruit cake and a large pot of tea snuggled under a tea cosy. For me this was food for the soul, simple and true.

All of my Dad's family cooked, They were wonderful and creative making the very best of home grown and local ingredients. I can remember *Taid* (Welsh for grandfather) plucking pheasants in the shed, and *Nain* roasting them with onions and chestnuts. Vegetables were dug fresh from the garden, rinsed and then prepared for lunch or supper, a delicious meal that included things like sweet runner beans, glazed carrots that tasted like honey, potatoes that had the texture of fondant and cabbage, shredded

My father with his father Iorweth outside the house Hyfrydle in Corris.
Also pictured are my dad's grandparents and Aunts

fine and cooked to perfection, finished with a little salty butter and black pepper.

My Dad had left home from a small village in Wales to the big city. Having gone to agricultural college he found work in the dairy industry just outside London which is where he met my mum. Later he would become the owner of a successful dairy in Caerphilly making cheese and butter; you could say 'the boy did good'.

My first real memories of life with them was in Porthcawl – picnics on the beach, foraging for mushrooms after Dad's game of golf, and picking blackberries all day for jams, pies and crumbles. Dad would often bring home fish and game in season. We ate simply, but I can remember everything, pikelets for tea (little pancakes) on a Sunday, rissoles made with left over roast meat on a Monday, macaroni cheese, milk jelly, pasties, faggots and peas were all typical dishes we ate during the week. Saturday was special; I can remember the first exotic food I ate, it was a Vesta Curry. It came in a box and was dried. You added water, heat, waited for it to thicken, and served it with rice. For some reason we loved it. I suppose because it was so very different to anything we had ever tasted. We all love curries now, but make them ourselves with fresh ingredients.

Growing up on our family farm was an inspiration. By my mid-teens I had started my love affair with food, yet never thought of it as anything but a hobby. We had a wonderful vegetable, fruit and herb garden, rich with seasonal produce. Little did I realise that I was so in tune with this natural larder that I would plan dishes ahead knowing what would soon be available. I experimented with flavours and textures, made preserves, jellies, pickles and chutneys. In the summer, we had an abundance of berries; my mother would make rhubarb and strawberry pie with the lightest buttery sweet pastry. We as a family have a sweet tooth, so I would always make lots of cakes and puddings. I cooked all the food for my dad's fortieth birthday party; I was sixteen years old and tackled my first whole poached, dressed salmon. I made hollandaise sauce, steamed asparagus and new potatoes with parsley and lemon all from my Mum's Cordon Bleu magazine.

A few years later, I left the farm for London. I started to earn money cooking, and moved on to Châteaux in Belgium,

Switzerland and Paris. From restaurants, gastro pubs and catering to cooking for Andrew Lloyd Webber, I took with me all of those dishes, all that know-how passed on to me so generously from my family. I have been lucky enough to have worked in television and radio, sharing recipes and anecdotes with lots of people. These days I teach everything from beginners cookery to masterclasses for fish and game. Wales is such a beautiful place that people visit from all over the world, and with the best of ingredients, it gives me so much pleasure to offer them a 'taste of Wales'. It's amazing how everything seems to have come full circle; it's like getting in touch with my roots, confirming that everything I have learnt about food all started here with the soil, the seasons and the knowledge of others.

Caws Pobi

This is delicious and satisfying food made in an instant. Growing up with a family in the dairy business, there was always a good chunk of cheese in the refrigerator. My dad would make this supper treat on his favourite white and blue enamel tin plate.

Ingredients

75gm good-quality
    mature-type cheddar
Crusty bread to serve

Method

Grate the cheese directly onto a heat-proof plate – enamel or a Pyrex dish is good.
Preheat your grill until hot.
Place the plate under the grill, and allow the cheese to melt and bubble.
Remove carefully with an oven cloth.
Place on a heat mat, and serve with crusty bread.
Serves: 1-2 people.

We have also added ingredients to this dish over the years, just like a pizza! Try adding soft cooked red onions, cherry tomato halves, cooked mushrooms, crispy bacon, or shredded sliced ham. Serve also with an accompanying salad and pickles.

Stuffed Shoulder of Local Lamb

Ingredients

1 shoulder of lamb, boned

Sea salt and pepper

Good bunch of mixed herbs such as
basil, parsley, chives, mint and thyme

150gm almonds

100gm pine nuts

4 cloves garlic

4 tbsp olive oil

2 chopped preserved lemons, or 8 large
green olives, stoned and chopped

1 tsp ground cinnamon

½ tsp ground cumin

Lamb still remains a firm favourite in our house today. Lamb is such a versatile meat, and I have discovered lots of ingredients that compliment its rich, sweet flavour, from samphire and laverbread, to stronger Mediterranean influences such as olives, capers and anchovies.

Laverbread (or *bara lawr* in Welsh) is an edible seaweed, and a traditional Welsh delicacy which is harvested from the Gower coastline.

Method

Lay the shoulder out on a board and season well with sea salt and pepper.

Place the herbs, almonds, pine nuts, garlic, olive oil, lemon and spices in a food processor to combine.

Spread over the meat, leaving a border all the way around.

Carefully roll up and secure with string. Wrap in oiled foil, and bake in a preheated oven at 180°c/gas mark 4 for about 2 hours.

Remove from the heat, open the foil, baste and return to the oven until golden – another 20 minutes.

Take the lamb out of the oven, and leave it to rest for 20 minutes before carving. Serve with pressed potato and leek terrine and roasted tomatoes. While the lamb is roasting, prepare the tomatoes. Cut them in half, and place them in a roasting tin. Drizzle with olive oil, sprinkle with salt and pepper. Stud with a spike of garlic, and finish with a little sugar. Roast slowly for about 2 hours, serve with the lamb.

Serves: 4 people.

Blackberry Pudding

The end of my childhood summers would always be marked by a few blackberry picking excursions to the countryside near the seaside town of Porthcawl. We would return home with bags of fat berries; hands and mouths black from the juice. My mother would freeze many of them in bags, so we could enjoy them throughout the coming winter months. Some would be turned into jams, crumbles and pies. One instant pudding is this, which is from my dad's childhood, but I have given it a grown up touch with some berry liqueur.

Ingredients

1 cup/350gm caster sugar
1/2 cup/5 fl oz berry liqueur- black currant, blackberry, damson, raspberry
750gm blackberries or mixed berries
12 slices of 'rustic' bread, slightly dry
Sauce glaze
250gm dark berries
150gm sugar
1/3 cup berry liqueur

Method

Place the sugar, liqueur or water and berries in a large pan, heat together until the fruit comes to a boil. Turn down the heat, stir gently until the fruits are soft but still hold their shape, remove from the heat. Take an 8 inch spring-form cake tin, line with clingfilm. Place a layer of bread on the base, followed by 1/3 of the berries and juice. Then repeat with another layer of bread, then berries and juice. Top with the remaining bread and berries.

Place a plate over the top that just fits inside the tin, place a weight on top and refrigerate.

Make the sauce glaze by boiling the sugar, fruit and liqueur. Boil until the liquid has a syrupy consistency and coats the back of a spoon. Remove from the heat and pass through a sieve to remove any pips. To serve the next day, turn the berry mould out onto a serving plate, peel off the clingfilm. For a little drama at the end, pour the sauce glaze over the pudding at the table. Serve in wedges with cream, Greek style yoghurt or crème fraiche.

Serves: 6 people.

Calon Diwylliant Cymru

Prif ganolfan hanes teulu Cymru
Arddangosfeydd o drysorau'r genedl
Llawysgrifau, archifau a chyhoeddiadau cyfoes
Archif Genedlaethol Sgrin a Sain Cymru
Gwefan sylweddol
Café a Siop

The Heart of Welsh Culture

Wales's premier family history centre
Exhibitions of the nation's treasures
Manuscripts, archives and contemporary publications
National Screen and Sound Archive of Wales
Extensive website
Café and Shop

**LlGC
NLW**

Llyfrgell Genedlaethol Cymru
The National Library of Wales
Aberystwyth

Noddir gan
Lywodraeth Cynulliad Cymru
Sponsored by
Welsh Assembly Government

www.llgc.org.uk

Hazel Thomas

I have no doubt that my childhood living on the farm, which was also the village pub, influenced my choice of career as a professional chef. I grew up living and working the land with the animals as part of that lifestyle. We would sell the milk to the Milk Marketing Board as well as utilize it in the home for cooking and making butter and cheese. Butter was produced by skimming off the cream from the milk and then, using a crude butter churning glass jar on a rotating instrument, my great aunt would sit for hours by the open fire as she churned the milk through the many stages before it became butter. Eggs would be free range of course, so fresh they would still be warm as you collected them. Every year we kept one pig which could be fed and fattened in time for the autumn months when it would be slaughtered. The dead pig would hang in the cellar along with the casks of ale and crates of beer until it was ready for curing. The sides were then hung from the rafters in the *gegin fach* (small kitchen). The head was boiled with other parts of the animal to make brawn, and we would eat the tenderloin that we referred to as *y llygoden*, (Welsh for mouse) the evening of the kill. I always remember how tasty that part of the pig was and more importantly how this joint needed to be eaten immediately because there was no fridge in the house.

Each autumn my mother Rita and great aunt Amy would produce elderflower wine from the freshly picked elder flowers which grew on the farm. I can recall one year in particular when I was about nine, that my mother, by mistake, fed the pig with the fermented fruit from the elderflower wine and this made the pig drunk. Many of the local farmers heard about this and descended on the farm, gathering around the pig sty to witness a drunken pig chasing its tail. It was an even better story repeated later in the pub with a pint of the real ale drawn from an old fashioned wooden cask. Come September we would harvest the blackberries which grew in the fields and

these would then be turned into freshly baked blackberry pies, a treat to look forward to each year. Vegetables were grown in the small garden with apples and pears grown in the tiny little orchard next to the hay barn. We also grew grapes and tomatoes in a little greenhouse. Travellers through the village would probably have been amazed to find outstretched hessian sacks with onions and shallots laid on them to dry out in the sun outside the pub. Half-term holiday in October was potato week as this was the time to pick and harvest all the potatoes grown on the farm. These hardier and larger potatoes would be our staple food for the cold winter months to come. Living and eating with the seasons has taught me the importance of food in relation to health and well-being.

Caring for the animals was also an integral part of life for me and I can recall having to go with my great uncle to churn the mangles into fodder for the cows. Food was grown and utilized for animal as well as human consumption. This was the way of life for the family which was of course typical of the farming way of life in West Wales. When it was sheep shearing time all the neighbouring farmers would get together working from one farm to the next until all the work was completed. At the end of the shearing a large piece of tarpaulin, laid out for packing the wool, would be used for everyone to sit on as they ate home made Welsh cakes and sandwiches with cups of hot sweet tea poured from an old fashioned metal caddy or *stên*.

That was my humble beginning, and thanks to a great Chef called Doug Harvey who recognised the potential in me, at seventeen, I embarked on a career in the catering industry by attending a three-year full-time professional chef's course at Westminster College, in Vincent Square, London. On completion of the training, I was fortunate to be offered two jobs, one was at the House of Lords, which I turned down, and the other was at the Dorchester Hotel which I accepted. Anton Mosimann was the Head Chef at the time and had only recently been appointed to that position. I was the first young female chef to be employed by him. He influenced my life considerably,

Me at 2 years old in my mother's arms with great Uncle Jack Dan and great Aunt Amy

and not just because of his culinary expertise. I was around during the period he introduced *Cuisine Naturelle* to the world. It was pioneering at the time, when most dishes were Classical and required lots of butter and cream to finish them off. I can categorically vouch for his being the major influence for a healthier style of cooking and eating on a professional level back then in the late 70's. His work clearly influenced how I would regard healthy eating later on in my life, especially when I became the guest cook for HTV (Welsh Television Company) in 1986 for a series on healthy eating for a healthier heart.

I left the Dorchester in the summer of 1979 to work at the British Transport Hotel Tregenna Castle in St Ives, Cornwall. This was for financial necessity more than anything else and it meant that I could at last start to save money and buy my first car. The same car almost cost me my life in 1981 when I experienced a near fatal car accident and was forced home to live with my family again in West Wales. The accident meant that I was too weak to return to catering immediately, so I found lighter work with a young graduate who was about to open a business in my home town. Although this meant a change of career, my love for cooking never left me, and becoming my own boss allowed me the time to attend university as a mature student where in 1996 I gained a degree in Welsh. It was this academic study of Welsh history, language and culture which helped me to embrace my own family roots and nurtured my understanding of my Celtic roots.

The turning point and first step for my return into the catering industry came in 1998 when I helped the Lampeter Chamber of Trade organise their first Food Festival. It proved to be a great success and I was co-ordinator for the event for 7 years. In 1999 when the Festival was moved to the grounds of Lampeter University, HRH the Prince of Wales came to open the event. My experiences having co-ordinated the Festival ultimately prompted me to become a food consultant and event organiser. I now enjoy a variety of opportunities working within the food sector. I am also back living at the home

My great grandmother (centre) with my grandmother on the left next to great Uncle Jack Dan and great Aunt Amy next to the tall gentleman who is unknown

that I grew up in, where I have been since my mother's death in 1992. It has been my mother's family home since 1893, and my children are the fifth generation to live there. As a village pub and farmhouse, it was the focal point of village life deep in the heart of West Wales. My great grandfather Danny Davies had been a game keeper at the Highmead Estate, living in one of the estate cottages, but with the advent of the motor car he was asked to move so that the chauffer could live close to the estate. That is when he moved to what is now my family home. Danny Davies sadly committed suicide in 1905 leaving my great-grandmother with seven children to care for. When I was born in 1957, my grandmother Ann Sarah, great aunt Amelia Margareta and great uncle Jack Daniel were still alive and living at the property with my parents. Thankfully, there was enough room still at the Inn and a year later my mother gave birth to twin boys. They were named Clifford and Jeffrey after the two doctors who assisted at the births.

During a BBC Wales radio series in 2008 called 'Look up your Genes', I was presented with information regarding my great grandfather's suicide. This enabled me to understand the pain and sorrow they must all have experienced due to his untimely death. Looking back however and growing up as I did with the senior members of my clan, I now realize why the family had been so guarded about certain elements of family history. Great Uncle Walter emigrated to Ohio in the 1920's but all I have remaining are a few photographs of him and a letter he wrote to my great grandmother in 1931.

These influences are all part of who I am today, and my food journey has taken me from *Cawl* to Caviar. I feel privileged to be living in a home with such an interesting history, and I am blessed to be living in an area of Wales which is abundant with fresh food, from the Ceredigion coastline right across the Teifi valley as far as the Cambrian Mountains. My hope is that the recipes I demonstrate at the Smithsonian Folk Life Festival will tempt people to visit Wales, and feel the magic of my homeland.

Roasted Tenderloin of Pork with Vegetable Roulade

This is my very own modern take on the tenderloin of Pork which is far removed from the days when my mum would just cook it in a pan with some onions and eggs.

Method

Pre heat your oven to 190°C - 375°F or Gas 5. Cover a Swiss roll tin with parchment paper, and grease lightly. Squeeze out as much of the water as possible from the cooked spinach, and chop it. Slowly sweat off the grated carrot in some butter in a pan. Place the chopped spinach into the pan with the carrots and warm through. Remove the saucepan from the heat before adding the egg yolks one at a time stirring continuously to avoid the eggs from scrambling. Whip the egg whites until stiff and add to the mixture. Add nutmeg and season.

Turn the mixture out evenly onto the tray, and cook in the oven for about 15-20 minutes or until the egg looks slightly browned on the surface and springs back to the touch. Remove from the paper and roll up in a clean sheet of paper wrapped inside a damp cloth.

When the roulade is cool, fill the centre with vegetables of your choice. Bind them together using crème fraiche or a yoghurt cheese mixture (if serving the roulade cold). Alternatively, use warm spiced apples if you prefer a warmer accompaniment to the pork tenderloin.

To roast the tenderloin of pork, simply roll the tenderloin in some olive oil and seasoning. Seal the meat in a hot frying or sauté pan until the meat is brown then transfer into a hot oven to cook until the meat is ready. Depending on the size of the meat, it normally takes less than 20 minutes. You can remove the meat from your pan and make a quick simple sauce by de-glazing the pan with some cloudy apple juice and thickening it with a little butter and seasoning to taste.

Serves: 4 people.

Ingredients

For the Vegetable Roulade

500gm Fresh spinach or 250gm pre-cleaned spinach cooked and drained

2 carrots, grated and a mixture of vegetables of your choice for the filling

30gm butter

4 eggs, separate yolks from the whites

Salt and pepper to taste

Nutmeg

Welsh Lamb & Leek
Cawl

Cawl is considered to be the national dish of Wales and each region of Wales has its own variation on this wonderfully wholesome dish. My version is from Ceredigion and favours the shoulder of lamb due to the sweet flavours of the meat. I have included the Welsh translation for the ingredients list.

Ingredients

8 carrots / moron
8 med potatoes / tatws
1 small swede / sweden
3 small leeks / cennin
3 parsnips / panas
500gm shoulder of lamb / cig oen
salt and pepper / halen a phupur
a bouquet garni or stock cube / stoc llysiau

Method

Cover the shoulder of lamb with water, a little salt and the bouquet garni. (You could make your own by tying some fresh herbs inside a layer of leek). Bring to a boil then simmer for a good 1-2 hours. Remove the meat, and set aside to cool before removing it from the bone. Cut the meat into small pieces.

Add the vegetables to the stock, starting with the hardest root ones first. Leave your cleaned and sliced leeks to the very end as they do not require much cooking. Season to taste with salt and pepper. You might need to add some vegetable stock powder or a bouillon cube if you feel the *cawl* requires more flavour.

Return the meat to the *cawl* and heat through before serving with crusty bread and Welsh cheese.

Serves: 6 people

Laverbread and Cockle Quiche
with cruciferous salad

To make the pastry, sift the flour and salt and rub in the butter to resemble breadcrumbs. Add enough cold water or egg to form the dough. Set aside to rest. Use this to line your quiche dish.

Method

Slice the onion and cut the red and yellow peppers into even-sized pieces.Sweat gently in some olive oil until soft but not coloured. Set aside to cool while you make the pastry.

Roll out the pastry and line your quiche dish.

Mix 1pt of milk with three eggs and whisk thoroughly. Place the cooled vegetables on your pastry lined quiche dish. Distribute the drained cockles evenly over the vegetables. Distribute your grated cheese on top of the cockles. Add laverbread to the milk and eggs and pour immediately into the dish.

Cook for about 30-40 mins or until set at 190°C 375°F or Gas 5.

The cruciferous salad is made by shredding a mixture of white and red cabbage.

Add to this some shredded and blanched savoy cabbage. Mix the three cabbages together and stir in a dressing made from olive oil, cider vinegar, some clear honey, salt and pepper.

Finish by adding some crème fraiche to this to make a healthy mayonnaise-style dressing.

Serves: 4 people.

Ingredients

1 red onion
1 red pepper
1 yellow pepper
½ tin or 2 dessert spoons of
    fresh laverbread
1 jar of cockles or 2oz fresh
100gm strong cheese
For the pastry
200gm self-raising flour
100gm butter
Salt
Cold water or 1 egg

Mwynhewch y blas, blaswch gynnyrch Sir Benfro

Take pleasure in the taste, discover Pembrokeshire produce

www.pembrokeshire.gov.uk/foodanddrink

Gareth Johns

There's no nicer sound for a chef than the clink of plates and glasses with happy chatter from the dining room, and no better sight than empty plates! The idea of using food for sharing pleasure and enjoyment has been the driving force behind my love of all things culinary from an early age. It's a well worn cliché, but for me it really did begin on grandma's knee! Grandma's cookery was good, traditional 'plain fare' – roasts, puddings, pies and wonderful baking. Early dishes included rice pudding (still a great favourite), cooked breakfast – welcome to a crash course in timing! – and lobscouse, or 'lobby' as we called it, a rib-sticking dish of left-over roast trimmings, potatoes and onions, all of which seemed to find favour with the recipients.

My 'Road to Damascus' occurred when visiting a work colleague of Mum's near Milton Keynes, where my parents were teaching at the time. As with most children, I found the visit boring, and in desperation I searched the bookshelves for something to stave off my murderous thoughts. My eye alighted upon Robert Carrier's 'Great Dishes of the World'. I was amazed and captivated by the passion and enthusiasm of his writing about my favourite subject – food – and the die was cast! I was going to be a chef!

After a brief flirtation with the (right side of the) law and the military, I was able to begin as a chef in industrial catering, which certainly gave me a rapid insight into customer satisfaction. You try placating a big, hairy docker who doesn't like his beef stew! I wangled my way into the job by saying I'd been in charge of an Army kitchen, which technically was true, but what I didn't tell them was that it was only for a week whilst carrying out adventure training in Snowdonia! Fortunately, I'm a quick learner, and memories of Grandma helped too. She was a demon shopper, believing very firmly that if you began with the best, you would get a good end product, and that you got what you paid for – advice which has stood me in good stead through my life – and not only in catering. After the dock, I went to college for my 706/1, and I got a fascinating job as a relief chef for Social Services – a kind of 'have-whisk-will-travel'

My great grandfather (centre) fishing for lobster off Dale Rocks

job which taught me to be able to hit the ground running and produce lunch for forty to fifty people using only a potato peeler and half a pound of mince.

Relatives had bought a small private hotel in Cornwall some years previously and had decided to spread their wings and convert a lovely old Water Mill to a restaurant. They had a Head Chef, and asked me if I would like the *Sous-Chef* position. I served my notice, packed my car and was heading down the A30 to Penzance before you could say 'Nouvelle Cuisine!' The chef was a mad Scouser called Deryck, who I still keep in touch with. He trained at the now infamous Adelphi Hotel in Liverpool, which was one of the World's great hotels, and was heavily influenced by John Tovey, of Miller Howe. Deryck was (and is) an excellent chef. He taught me additional and better skills, reinforced the quality message, and brought in consistency. Deryck's food is equally good if he's cooking for one, one hundred, or one thousand. It was here that my love affair with bread began. We baked our own rolls and loaves, and I worked the 'shop shift' in a local bakery to learn more (and become a fiendish Cornish pasty crimper!). I kept the kitchen in line with standards and profitability until the owners decided on a change of direction to a more casual 'brasserie' style, a bold move in the early 80's. After long discussion, we decided to part company. I wanted to continue in 'fine-dining'.

Then to the Lake District, a country house hotel on the shores of Ullswater, with a chef seeking recognition for his food and working under the influence of the French Masters, in particular Michel Guerard. Here I learned more new techniques and precision, both in execution and presentation. It was the first time I'd ever thought of eyebrow tweezers as an essential part of a chef's toolkit! It was also my first introduction to life as a member of a 'brigade', and learning the rules of the jungle, both written and unwritten. The pastry Chef, Pete McDougall was an ethereal baker, but beware if you annoyed him- the beef you had slow-roasting during the afternoon 'split' would become mysteriously burnt to a crisp, without the thermostat leaving 160°C. It was only later he confessed to sneaking in, turning it up and then down again before the unfortunate's return!

Scotland the brave was next to offer itself up as my culinary classroom, and it

was here that I first really came into contact with local produce. Up until then, it was largely about the technique of the Chef, and buying produce from Rungis Market near Paris, because that's what all the top chefs did.

Seasonality and provenance were unheard of to a large extent, but for me Scotland changed all that. Beef, salmon, lamb, vegetables, fruit and cheeses were proudly displayed on menus, and suddenly it all made sense to me. I worked in a number of restaurants and hotels in Edinburgh and the borders; some better than others, and some of International renown, but a strong sense of place was common to all. Even Ron Reglinski, the Head Chef at The Thistle Hotel, still cooking at sixty three, regarded himself as far more of a Scot than a Pole! Slow Food had barely begun in Italy, but my interest in its principles had already been awakened, albeit unwittingly at that stage. My next move was propitiated by more personal circumstances, the break-up of a long term relationship, as I suddenly found myself free to attend finishing school. London calling!

By now I had worked my way around the various sections of a kitchen to a high standard, but as the ultimate idea was a place of my own I felt I needed to know more about the management side of kitchens, The spectre of the Tower Thistle hotel arose – 826 bedrooms, 5 kitchens, and nearly 80 cooks! – If I couldn't learn kitchen management here...? One telephone call and a train journey later I was in the office of Ian MacDonald, the BTH-trained martinet who was the Executive Chef of the hotel. What could I offer him? he asked. Loyalty, I replied. He must have liked the idea- I got the job! Chef, as he was always known, ran the hotel kitchens with a rod of iron and meticulous attention to detail. After the initial culture shock, I settled down to learn from the Master. Despite his demeanour, he was very easy to work for, because he never varied from day to day in his moods or his standards, a lesson worth learning indeed. To keep my hand in, I cooked around London as well, working as a tournant for the brilliant Alastair Little at the height of his fame, when the kitchen ran on self-discipline, love of food, and

Lyndale (left) The Post Office & Village Shop next to Rock Cottage Herbrandston. The family homes

hours of banter amongst some very talented cooks indeed.

I ended my time in London on a real high, working at its grandest old lady-The Ritz as sous-chef. During my touring years, my parents had moved back home to Pembrokeshire, and I was summoned home one weekend for a family conference. Dad's health was failing, and a proposition was put forward that we should go into business together as a family. We agreed, and began to look for suitable premises. It seemed like every pub in West Wales was for sale at the time, and after looking at hundreds we plumped for the Red Lion, in the wonderfully named village of Llanfihangel-Nant-Melan, Radnorshire. Having been promised vacant possession, it was like a 'Carry-On' movie as we moved in at one end and the previous occupants went out of the other! It had always been the plan to come back to Wales, and here I was with a free hand for the first time. I decided from day one that the menu would be firmly based on our wonderful Welsh produce, would be short and manageable and would change as things ran out. People began to talk about the little white-washed roadside inn. The first guide book to arrive was Egon Ronay, then the AA, then the Good Food Guide and Michelin weighed in. We were in the first batch of 'gastro-pubs' rewarded by Michelin at the outset, and won awards from the Taste of Wales. Sadly, Dad's health continued to deteriorate, and in 2000 we sold up, and my parents began a well- earned retirement. I had by this time also got involved with the fledgling Welsh Culinary Team, and Arwyn Watkins, a fellow team member knew of a hotel in Machynlleth where the owners were seeking to recruit a new Head Chef. I visited the Wynnstay Hotel, and I fell in love. I've been here ever since, and in March 2008, my brother Paul and I bought the freehold from Charles and Sheila Dark. We are now the proud owners of the Wynnstay where we offer short menus of fresh food, following the Slow Food principles (I'm the Slow Food's Ambassador Chef for Wales). Food waste is cut to a minimum - I hate waste, and there are too many hungry people in the world! Our philosophy is fairness, consistency, and above all, a pleasure in sharing, in hearing the clink and chatter and seeing those empty plates- and isn't that where we came in?

Crusader's Salmon

This dish is called Crusader Salmon in honor of the Guardian Angel at St. Mary's church, Herbrandston. The legend has it that the Guardian Angel was a Crusader who spread his wings to protect the service men of Herbranston as they went to war. The idea of using the ginger, spice and citrus fruit was popularized by the returning soldiers from the East.

INGREDIENTS

1 square buttered foil 8x8 inch

170gm fillet of salmon

Salt, pepper, mace

Sprig rosemary

2-3 slices of root ginger

Splash of dry white wine

Few slices of citrus fruit (as available)

Method

1. Season the foil lightly, and then add the rosemary and ginger. Place salmon on foil, topped with the citrus fruit, wine and more seasoning.
2. Fold foil into a parcel, bake in hot oven for 10-12 minutes depending on size and thickness of salmon.
3. Open parcels at the table in front of diners.

Serves: Recipe has been given per portion.

Katt Pie

This is a traditional Welsh dish which has its roots in Pembrokeshire. It was the speciality at the Templeton Hiring Fair held in November each year. They were traditionally eaten as you walked around the fair, pie in hand.

MAKE DOUGH

200gm flour
100gm fat half lard/half butter
Salt
Cold water

FILLING

50gm currants
50gm soft brown sugar
200gm lean minced lamb
Salt & freshly ground black pepper

Method

Mix all the ingredients together and fill your pies. Glaze with milk.

Bake 35-40 minutes at 190°c/375°f/gas 5 until golden brown. Cooking time will be a little less for the small individual pies.

Serves: yields 1 large or 12 small pies.

Cockle & Smoked Bacon Chowder

This is a creation that I developed during my many regular demonstrations at the Swansea Market Cockle Festival, which sadly no longer takes place. Penclawdd Cockles are still available at Swansea and Llanelli Markets and are widely recognized as being the best in the World.

INGREDIENTS

200gm (shelled weight) Penclawdd cockles, cooked
2 thick rashers smoked streaky bacon
1 small onion, diced
4 medium potatoes, peeled, cooked and diced
Salt, pepper & chopped parsley
1/2pt fish stock and 1/2pt milk (or all milk)
25gm Welsh butter

Method

In a heavy-bottomed pan fry the onion and bacon in the butter until soft.

Add the potatoes and liquids, and bring to simmering.

Add the cockles and heat through.

Do not boil, as this will make the cockles go tough.

Season to taste and finish with parsley

Serves: 4 people.

www.visit.
carmarthenshire
.gov.uk

UNITED KINGDOM

SOUTH WEST WALES

Anthony Evans

I was born in Gorslas a small village in Carmarthenshire. My family roots on my mother's side are from a farming and coalmining background. As a result of this, my earliest memories of hunting for food stem from the hard times which occurred during the 1984 mining strike, I learnt to eat the food that was available. I became accustomed to hunting and sourcing my own food, assisting my father during hunting sessions for wild game and fish. This was the seed which, at the tender age of eleven prompted me to become a Chef. I refer, of course, to a very basic form of cooking at grass roots level, to that rare breed of hunter-gatherer who is able to fend for himself and others, by living off the land. Coming from Carmarthenshire meant that I was blessed in terms of river habitat and wild life. As a child I had a bus pass and I took every advantage of this free mode of transport by regularly going fishing and hunting with my dogs and ferrets, much to the disdain of all the other passengers. The return journey laden with dead rabbits, live ferrets and the occasional salmon was most entertaining for the passengers to witness. I cared very little about the pungent smell I was trailing in my wake.

My fondest memories from childhood are learning how to fish and hunt with my father as my teacher. Hunting started at the very young age of six. We would go hunting for rabbits with just a dog and a ferret, without any guns. The dog would mark the holes and then these would be covered with nets. We would then put down the ferret and wait for the rabbit to make his escape into our nets. The rabbits would be killed by my father or me, using a rabbit punch to the back of the neck, which of course would be quick and humane. The dog would only be used if we were hunting with guns, to flush out and retrieve our catch.

When I was about four years old I went fishing with my father, and I managed to hook an eel. I took the eel proudly home and wanted to keep it as a pet, but my mother would not allow it. It

was skinned and cooked for supper. On another occasion, when I was very young and which also highlights my bad losing nature, my sister and I (along with both parents) had gone fishing. My sister caught a trout and I was so angry that I decided to spend a penny in the river right in the spot where my sister was fishing. To my horror, and as I was doing so, she managed to catch another trout. I am happy to say, however, that I have now matured somewhat and practise the art of fishing and shooting to a very high professional standard.

It was no surprise that I left school at sixteen and attended a course at a local catering college. Once I had completed the course I left for London, in search of a career as a chef. The world was my oyster in many ways, and I started my career at the Down Hall Country Hotel on the Hertfordshire Estate. I was overwhelmed by the live game on the estate which ranged from pheasants to deer, ducks and millions of rabbits. Each morning on my way to work I took great delight in counting as many rabbits as I could. No one was allowed to catch any of this wonderful live game available until the morning that the groundsman insisted that I bring my ferrets up to the estate to do a cull. We were not allowed to use guns due to the residents from the hotel wandering around the 110 acre grounds. We did manage, however, to catch 147 rabbits on our first hunt. We were forced to retire because both ferrets were exhausted. The rabbits were then taken to Burrow Market where we sold them all for a £1 each. In 1996 that was a bargain, bearing in mind that the average price of a rabbit in those days was around £7 each to purchase in London. You would have thought that our initial cull would have made something of a difference to the game population, but to my horror as I strolled down the drive on my way home from work, it was yet again carpeted with live rabbits. My time at Down Hall came to an end a year later when I decided to move on and I found a job at the Flemings Hotel in Mayfair. My time at the Flemings was great, but as they say, 'you can take the boy out of Wales, but you can't take Wales out of the boy'. My *hiraeth* (longing for home) was

Me 16 years of age pictured with an 8lb salmon caught on the river Towy

getting the better of me, so I moved closer to home and ended up in Bath working at the Bath Spa Hotel for a year and a half. My experiences of working and catering for the many celebrities who stayed there remain very special in my heart. Names like Pavarotti, Take That, Robbie Williams, John Paul Getty, Bill Gates and John Major were a few of them. The list goes on and on, but my favourite memory was sitting in the hotel sauna one day when Boyzone came in, I did not recognize any of them! I was unaware that my colleagues in the kitchen had rubbed Tabasco sauce into my swimming trunks and were watching me on the CCTV monitor from reception. During my conversation with Boyzone, I felt a very warm burning feeling from inside my trunks and had to run out very quickly from the sauna and wash myself down in the shower, having already embarrassed myself by suggesting to Boyzone that I had assumed they were staying at the hotel because they were actors appearing in the pantomime which was being performed locally.

In 1999 a chance conversation between my uncle and a member of a Welsh TV program enabled me to appear regularly on Welsh TV, cooking and sharing my knowledge of the catering world as well as my hunting and fishing experiences. I did this for two years and then progressed to doing a Welsh language program for Tanni Gray Thomson, Janet Street Porter and many other celebrities. My role became that of presenter as well as TV Chef, and I now appear regularly on my own Welsh cooking program aimed at the younger generation. This has enabled me to experience a wide range of foods from around the world. I enjoy demonstrating, and am asked to do this for various organizations throughout Wales. Just recently, my TV program called 'Stwffio' was nominated for two Welsh BAFTA's (The British Academy of Film and Television Arts) and one British BAFTA.

Life can seem a bit glamorous when your work allows you to travel as extensively as I do, but my feet are kept firmly on the ground thanks to my family roots and traditions. No matter what I do or where I go, coming home to that

Me with a 28½ lb Chum Salmon caught on the river Vedder in Canada

warm Welsh welcome is a constant reminder to me of how lucky I am to be a part of such an interesting clan of people.

I can actually trace my family back as far as the 17th Century My great, great grandmother, on my mother's side, was the last witch to be burnt at the stake. My mother told me that she was very well-known for her knowledge of healing herbs and would very often be asked to cure a variety of ailments. For instance, she produced a tea from a particular wild plant which would be beneficial for people with kidney problems. She also had a reputation for making a wonderful dandelion wine. My grandmother, on my father's side, who is also from a farming background, grew up on Llwynbrain Farm, which is located close to the National Botanic Garden of Wales. At one time it was one of the largest farms in the area. His mother was one of eleven children. One of her brothers, Jack, actually built a plane, using a Land Rover engine. He managed to fly the plane on the farm for a short distance of two fields before crashing down. He knew how to take off and fly, but had no idea of how to land the plane. He ended up in the hospital but the only thing that was broken was the plane. The story is still told today amongst the older generation. It would appear that this interest in mechanics has been passed down to my father who loves nothing more than to have his nose under the bonnet of a car or lorry. Jack's father, my great grandfather used to have one of the earliest milk rounds in the area. He would deliver milk from farm to farm on his horse and cart. So many of the old traditions have changed due to a more modern way of living and yet so much has been lost along the way. That personal touch handing out the milk farm to farm is so far removed from picking up a plastic bottle from the fridge at your local supermarket. I sincerely hope that stories such as these can be kept alive in the hearts of our children to pass on from generation to generation just as I am doing, and you are reading. We all have a story to tell.

Rabbit in a Champagne Dijon Mustard Sauce

Method

1. Pre-heat the oven to gas mark 5.
2. Skin and gut the rabbit then wash and cut into joints.
3. Chop the onion and garlic finely and sauté with the jointed rabbit in butter until the meat is golden brown.
4. Add the Dijon mustard and the champagne and reduce to half over a high heat.
5. Add the vegetable stock, bay leaf and lemon juice.
6. Transfer the contents into a casserole dish and place in the oven for 30 minutes or until juices are reduced to half.
7. Remove the dish from the oven and set over a hob on a low heat.
8. Add the cream and the chopped parsley and continue to stir well until the sauce comes to the boil.
9. Season well with salt and pepper and serve with game chips and wilted watercress.

Serves: 4 people.

INGREDIENTS

1 rabbit in the fur
1 whole onion
1 clove of garlic
1 tablespoon of Dijon mustard
60gm of butter
¼ pint of vegetable stock
1 bay leaf
Squeeze of lemon juice
½ pint of extra thick double cream
¼ pint of Champagne
Chopped parsley
Salt and pepper

Stuffed Breast of Duck Served with a Port and Wild Berry Jus

INGREDIENTS

1 duck breast
30gm of picked
    spinach leaves
30gm of Welsh
    goats cheese
30gm of shredded
    carrot
60gm of brown
    sugar
90gm butter
1 measure of port
90gm of mixed wild
    berries
60gm flour
6 sliced shallots
1 clove of garlic
¼ pint of duck stock
Orange zest
2 table spoons of
    olive oil
Cold water
Salt and pepper

Method

1. Pre-heat oven to gas mark 4.

2. Using a sharp knife make an incision in the middle of the duck breast to form a pocket on the inside and stuff the pocket with layers of picked spinach leaves, Welsh goats cheese and shredded carrot.

3. Tie the breast with a butchers cord ensuring that it secures the stuffing during cooking.

4. Score the breast with a knife.

5. Add the butter to a frying pan and sauté off the shallots, garlic and orange zest together.

6. Add the breast to the pan and seal the meat until golden brown.

7. Place the breast into a roasting tin and sprinkle with 1oz of brown sugar. Place in the oven for 15 minutes, checking after 10 minutes for colouration of meat.

8. Using the contents of the frying pan add the mixed wild berries and sauté for a further 2 minutes.

9. Add the stock and remaining sugar and reduce to half over a high flame.

10. Top up with a measure of port and bring to the boil.

11. In a separate dish mix together flour and cold water to form a milky substance. Gradually add to the boiling stock until a thick jus forms. Season with salt and pepper.

12. Serve with a sliced breast of duck and roasted vegetables.

Serves: recipe given is per portion.

Wild River Towy Salmon on a melody of laverbread and Welsh Seafood Mix

Method

1. Pre-heat oven on gas mark 6.
2. Cut a square piece of foil and place flat on a clean work surface. Place the fillet of salmon in the middle together with 60gm of butter, lemon juice, tarragon, salt, pepper and dry martini.
3. Fold the foil to form a parcel. Make an incision to allow steam to evaporate and place in the oven.
4. Meanwhile fry off the onion, garlic, smoked bacon and sliced mushrooms in the remaining butter.
5. Add the cockles and mussels and dry sherry, burning off all the alcohol.
6. Add the laverbread and mix thoroughly until the mixture comes to the boil. Season with salt and pepper.
7. On a clean plate scoop the seafood mixture into the middle, place the salmon on top and drizzle with the remaining juice left inside the foil parcel and serve.

Serves: recipe given is per portion.

INGREDIENTS

1 fillet of Towy salmon
120gm butter
½ onion finely chopped
60gm of laverbread
A small handful of Welsh cockles and mussels
2 button mushrooms
1 clove of garlic
1 measure of dry sherry
Smoked bacon
1 measure of dry martini
1 tsp of tarragon
1 tsp of lemon juice
Salt and pepper

Geraldine Trotman

My story begins at number 2 Christina Street, Old Tiger Bay – 1952, the year I was born. Our modest two-bedroom home stood at the top of a row of small terraced houses. We had no telephone, no TV or indoor bathroom. A call of nature in the middle of the night meant that you'd either have to brave the elements to use the outside toilet with the paraffin lamp, or use the enamel potty kept under one's bed. The tin bath hanging in the backyard would be brought in front of the fire where the water would be heated in galvanized buckets, for your weekly bath. My father was the lucky one who would bathe more regularly because of his demanding work on the dock as a boiler scaler. Heating came from the same coal fire with ovens on either side. Throughout the day puddings and stews were cooked on this open fire in the middle room. I always remember my mother, Irene Josephine Trotman, in her paisley pinafores. All women seemed to don this same attire, almost like a community uniform.

My father, Kenneth McKenzie Trotman, was born in 1906 on the island of St. Lucia. At the young age of 13 he became a stowaway galley boy searching for a new and better life. Our family has evidence that puts my father on the ship Gloria De Larrinaga, which travelled to Galveston, Texas where he was discovered and deported to Buenos Aires then sent to New York. New York then sent him back to the SS Urun where he was set ashore in Rio, Brazil. He told us many stories including how he came to travel to Cardiff's Docklands. Before I was born, my father was a seaman who traveled the world but never got close enough to see his homeland. Tiger Bay was now his home. He always mentioned the hospitality that he received from both black and white. And for this reason, he never looked back. My 2 brothers were 21 and 23 years my senior, so my mother described the news of the pregnancy with me as the biggest shock of her life and my father announced it was the best surprise ever! My parents were well known and

My parents, Irene and Kenneth Trotman long before my arrival.

respected in the community and before they passed away, celebrated their Platinum Anniversary – 70 years of marriage.

Irene, one of seven children, was the daughter of a Welsh woman named Maggie Rowlands and a West-Indian father named Thomas Nathaniel Darnell Emptage. Thomas, born in 1879, arrived in Wales from Barbados in the late 1800's and married Letitia Gordon in 1900 at St Mary's Church on Bute Street (a church that is still a focal point of the community today). Leticia died in September 1901 and my grandfather moved to Tonypandy in the valleys, (Pontypridd) to work in the coalmines where he met and married my grandmother Maggie Rowlands in 1902. My grandfather later returned to Tiger Bay with his three children, Hannah, Maud and Fitzgerald, and then went on to have another four children, Irene (my mother), Clara-May, Edith and Winifred. He ran a boarding house and a cook shop for seamen at 32 Maria Street. Granddad brought with him many culinary tips and a different style of cooking from his native Barbados and passed on many great recipes.

Cooking has always been a family tradition passed down from generation to generation, as far back as great granddad Emptage, a baker by profession back in his native land. In our home the influence of Welsh cuisine and spicy Caribbean dishes sent wonderful aromas throughout the whole house. Welsh cakes on the cast iron bake stone, plum and apple duffs, spotted dick, apple pie and many more delights complimented the main meal of chicken, peas and rice. Mrs. Trotman was well known for her black eyed peas and rice with a delicious chicken stew, granddad's chicken dumplings, sweet potatoes, yams, green bananas and whatever other Caribbean vegetables were readily available. Fish was always on the inexpensive menu on a Friday. Salt-fish was a favourite due to the cost and the fact that it could be stored without a fridge. Salt fish cakes, salt fish and corn meal dumplings were a real delight. I looked forward to seeing Tommy the fishmonger pull up his cart on wheels at the top of Christina Street where the women would gather to buy fresh fish gutted and filleted while they waited.

As humble a dwelling as we had at Christina Street, it was not unusual to

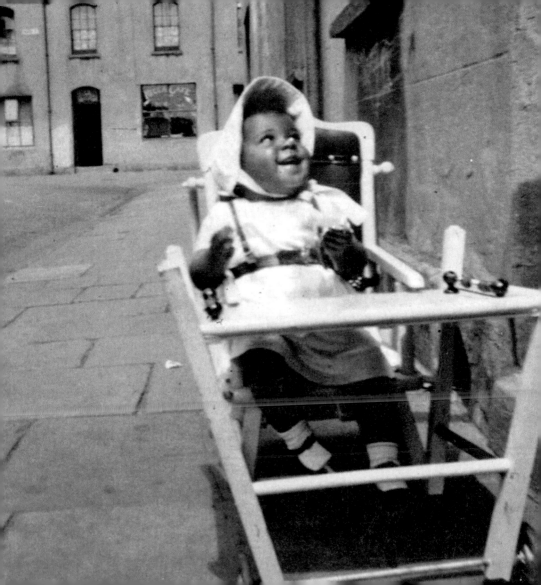

receive such visitors as The West Indian Cricket Team and Jomo Kenyatta, the first Prime Minister of Kenya. Hospitality was an important factor of the Trotman household. Good food and good music went hand in hand.

Tiger Bay was a unique community right in the heart of Cardiff Docklands, a community that was full of love and understanding. The Docks, a once bustling seaport, attracted seamen of many cultures to the world's major exporter of coal. My early childhood memories are of a community full of great characters and role models, and a great respect regardless of ethnicity, colour or culture. All adults in the community were addressed as Mr or Mrs, Aunty or Uncle. It was one huge extended family, a great melting pot, a place where Welsh women integrated and took husbands from every corner of the world. This was all taking place at a time where racial tensions were brewing all over the country and in fact the world and mixed marriages were frowned upon. Many women took on their new identity with pride although for some it was life without the blessing of their families. This cultural integration influenced these Welsh women's kitchens and whilst playing in the streets one could smell aromas from every nation.

Encouraged by my domestic science teacher, I went on to study hotel food and catering at the College of Food Technology & Commerce. On completing this I gained a few years experience in the trade before emigrating to Barbados, the homeland of my grandfather. The job I held dearest was as Food & Beverage Manager of the renowned Ocean View Hotel, one of the oldest hotels on the island with an excellent reputation for first class Bajan cuisine. This was an immense challenge for a twenty eight year old. It was here that I gained a wealth of knowledge from two wonderful women forty years my senior in an establishment that was highly commended for its first class authentic food. The experience was to forever change my relationship with food and drink. I discovered a whole new range of cooking methods and gained an insight into the many traditional

Geraldine outside her home, 2 Christina Street, Old Tiger Bay.

herbal remedies, an integral part of Caribbean life. It was here that I crafted my trade.

In 1984 after spending ten years in the Caribbean I returned to my home in Tiger Bay with my three daughters, Leanne, Jamilla and Ayaisha. Due to circumstances my love of the hospitality industry had to be put on the back burner. I worked for thirteen years for the National Health Service where I gained knowledge both positive and negative surrounding health issues. I spent a year at St David's Hotel & Spa in the Bay, and won the employee of the year award, before being made redundant. Family ties being important took me to my next role working for the charity 'Home-Start', which help's families going through difficult times. I was determined not to waste the skills I had acquired. Using my experiences I found ways to promote better health through many channels including the cooking course I developed to influence families away from convenience foods and encourage them to make simple, nourishing and inexpensive meals for their families, putting the soul back into the kitchen. "Come Shop With Me, Come Cook with Me" offers eight exciting weeks learning how to shop for and prepare tasty dishes for the whole family. I truly believe that a well-balanced diet promotes a healthy body and mind. The relationship between cultural heritage, migration and cuisine has left a unique legacy for the people with connections to Old Tiger Bay. Aromas and distant flavours bring back wonderful memories of a special place never to be forgotten. It is a privilege to be able to share the wealth of my knowledge about food which I have gained from my multicultural experiences and travels.

Salt Fish Balls

Method

1. Soak fish in cold water for approx 20-30mins.
2. Remove skin and place fish in saucepan, cover with water, bring to a boil and simmer for 15mins.
3. Drain water and allow to cool.
4. Flake the fish (making sure to remove all bones) into mixing bowl.
5. Process all seasoning (grate or finely chop)
6. Add to the fish.
7. Add flour, baking powder and enough water to make a medium batter.
8. Drop spoonfuls of the batter into hot deep oil and fry until golden brown.
9. Drain and serve.

Ingredients

200gm salt fish
200gm flour
2 tsp baking powder
2 onions
½ hot pepper (scotch bonnet)
Fresh parsley
Fresh thyme
Water to bind
Oil for frying

Serves: fish cakes cocktail size would make approx 30-35 enough for 6 people.

Granddads Chicken dumplings

Method

1. Grate onion. Add to minced chicken along with thyme and seasoning.
2. Place flour in mixing bowl, add eggs to make dough.
3. Roll out as thin as possible on lightly floured board.
4. Cut into small squares.
5. Place tsp of chicken mixture in the centre of each square.
6. Wet edges with a little water, bring together from each corner, and seal.
7. Drop the finished dumplings into sauce of choice and simmer for 20-30 mins.

Ingredients

150gm flour
2 eggs
1 onion
180gm minced chicken
Salt & black pepper
A little fresh thyme

My mother would say Granddads dumplings was a way of stretching the chicken. You could get away with serving a small piece of chicken and two of Granddads dumplings instead of the expected 2 reasonable sized pieces of chicken on the plate.

Serves: makes 8-10 chicken dumplings - enough for 4-5 people.

(2 per portion)

Split Pea, Leek & Potato Soup

Method

1. Roughly chop all vegetables.
2. Place in saucepan along with split peas.
3. Cover with water or stock and bring to the boil.
4. Season with salt and pepper.
5. Simmer until peas are soft.
6. Blend and serve hot.

Serves: 4 people.

Ingredients
½ cup of green split peas (soaked overnight)
1 small leek
3 medium potatoes
2 cloves garlic
1 onion
1 carrot
½ fresh chilli

Wales
Cymru

*...now where did I
leave my bike?*

An open invitation to explore Wales
www.visitwales.com

Ana Rees

I currently run the first Welsh Tea room in Patagonia, Argentina. It was opened in 1944 by my great grandmother, Dilys Owen. Dilys was born in Bangor at the end of the nineteenth century. She moved to Patagonia with her family at the beginning of the twentieth century because her brother was ill. The family bought a house called Plas y Coed which was situated in the middle of Gaiman village. Dilys was bought up here at the family home, and she later married a man called Dafydd Gwilym Rees who was from Aberdulais and who had settled in the village after going to Patagonia to look for his brother.

Sadly for Dilys, after only five years of marriage, her husband Dafydd died and she had to return to live with her family at Plas y Coed, with her three young children. Life was very poor for the family. They grew cherry trees and produced honey. The house was situated very close to the Chubut River, and on some occasions, following very heavy rains, the river would flood the family home and many of the village folk would lose all their possessions and crops.

After a while Dilys married again to another man from a Welsh family. Her new husband's family was from Colonia Sarmiento which was situated about four hundred kilometres to the south of Gaiman.

Dilys used to bake a lot, and she would share her many cakes amongst her friends. Each Saturday her friends would come together for afternoon tea. Dilys was famous for her baking, and her *cacen ddu* (black cake) was served at many a wedding in the village. In 1944, Dilys opened her home Plas y Coed as the first Welsh Tea House in Patagonia.

Since then of course there have been many visitors from all over the world to Plas y Coed. In 1977 Dilys died and her son Gwyn Rees my grandfather moved back to Plas y Coed with his wife Marta Roberts, to run the family business. My grandmother Marta Roberts was also from a Welsh family who had moved to Patagonia having come on the very first

Plas y Coed 1900

ship to arrive, the *Mimosa*. Marta's grandfather had helped to lay the very first bricks which formed the town of Rawson.

When Marta was eight her mother died, and she was moved to live with a South African family, who had moved to Comodoro Rivadavia, a southern state of Chubut. Sadly, she lost her first language Welsh, but she was the only Welsh woman in Patagonia to be able to speak the African language fluently. My mother was their only child, and because Marta had lost her Welsh, she was unable to teach her the language, although my grandfather was still a Welsh speaker.

I have many very fond memories of my visits to my grandparents' house. I learned how to cook the cakes that my grandmother used to cook on my many visits as a child to the tea house. I used to spend every summer holiday with my grandmother, and would of course get to help her out in the tea house. She would teach me, my sisters and my brother how to bake her famous cakes. I moved to live with her after my grandfather died in 1994. This gave me the opportunity of working with my grandmother and learning all about how to run the tea

room and she also taught me how to run the shop. My grandmother died in 2006, and my mother who now owns the house, decided to keep the family business open, I am now responsible for running the tea room. I have made some changes to the tea room, and in so doing made a decision to show all the many items of a Welsh connection which my grandmother had collected over the years. You will find on our walls many Welsh tea towels, some of which were bought by my grandparents and others which had been given to my grandparents by their friends. I have also added the ones that I had bought personally during my visits to Wales. There are also examples of the traditional Welsh love spoons hanging on the tea room walls. These have been specially commissioned for me from Patagonian wood. Whenever anyone calls at the tea room they will be greeted by the sound of Traditional Welsh songs. This is my way of sharing my Welsh Culture and traditions and I am very proud to share my family history and that of the Welsh to all the visitors who come to Gaiman and who visit the tea house.

The Cakes we serve in the tea room are what makes it so special for me as

My Great grandmother outside Plas y Coed

each of the recipes that I use has been handed down from my family. Each cake that we bake has its very own special history, and no Welsh tea would be complete without a plate of bread and butter with cheese and some scones with homemade jam.

Fortunately for me my great grandmother and great grandfather planted many fruit trees when they moved to this house and I am able to make jams from the plums, apricots, peaches, figs and apples which we grow here. These are all served in the tea room of course. I also make strawberry and raspberry jam from freshly picked berries which are grown at many farms in the valley. The choice of cakes on offer in the tea room range from the traditional Welsh cakes to apple tart, lemon tart, swiss roll with lemon cheese, chocolate cake with jam and cream, and the carrot cake. Some of the cake recipes were developed by other Welsh-women in the settlement. Each recipe has a history and each has its own requirements dependant on the ingredients that were available at the time. The cream tart for example is very tasty and was developed during a time when they would have been able to

get milk from the cows and turn this into butter and cream. This became a very popular cake in the area. The most famous cake of all is the *cacen ddu* or black cake. This was a recipe adapted from the traditional *bara brith* mixed with the Christmas pudding recipe. This recipe was developed more as a necessity than for any other reason, and was created by the Welsh-women of the settlement. They were looking for a food product which would last a long time in the event of flooding and when food became scarce. Each Welsh family in the area has their own recipe for this cake and each recipe is different in some way. Every year in April we hold an Agricultural Exposition in Gaiman and this has been a tradition here for the past 25 years. There are many different competitions held during the event and one of those is the famous Black Cake Competition. This year (2009) I won the first prize with my recipe for this cake.

I am now able to speak Welsh since learning the language in 2004. I felt that I needed to keep the Welsh traditions alive for the sake of the tea room and my family history and I feel that the language is the most important part of the Welsh culture. I was able to follow the Welsh language courses which are available in Patagonia and then once I felt confident enough I asked for a scholarship to attend the intensive Welsh language course at Lampeter University in West Wales. I also wanted to be able to teach Welsh back in Patagonia and so after the summer of 2006 studying at Lampeter, I returned to Patagonia and started teaching Welsh to adult learners. I have continued with my studies for personal improvement and I am currently studying my degree in Welsh through the internet. As well as running the tea room I also teach Welsh classes and I currently run three different courses with about forty students all learning Welsh. I am proud of my heritage and my Welsh family roots and I am now able to share the gift of my language with others who feel as passionate as I do about Wales and the Welsh. It is an honour for me to be a part of the Smithonian Folk Life Festival in 2009 when Wales is the guest nation. The link between Patagonia and Wales is as firm today as it has ever been.

When this book went to print Ana Rees had reached the preliminary round of the Welsh Learner of the Year competition at the National Eisteddfod of Wales.

Scones

Method

1. Mix the butter, with the egg, the yogurt and the sugar, then add the dry ingredients all together.
2. Do not knead too much. Roll out the dough with a rolling pin and cut out the scones with a pastry cutter.
3. Place the scones on a greased baking tin and bake in the oven which has been pre-heated to 200°C 400°F Gas 6 and cook them for about 25 minutes.

Ingredients

1 kg flour
4 teaspoons baking powder
1 teaspoon salt
200gm butter
1 egg
200gm yogurt
150gm sugar

This mixture will normally make about 35 scones. (depending on the size of your cutter)

Centigrade	Fahrenheit	Gas Mark
110	225	1/4
130	250	1/2
140	275	1
150	300	2
170	325	3
180	350	4
190	375	5
200	400	6
220	425	7

Pice ar y maen (pica bach)

Ingredients

1 kg flour
1 cup of sugar
2 teaspoons of baking powder
1 pinch of salt
1 pinch of nutmeg
1 pinch of cinnamon
1 cup of raisins
1 cup of butter
Milk
1 egg

Method

Mix all the dry ingredients first and then add the egg and milk.

This should produce a soft mixture.

Roll out on a board dusted with flour to ¾ inch thick.

Cut into rounds. Cook on a heated greased griddle pan until brown on both sides.

This mixture will normally make around 60 Welsh Cakes (depending on the size of your cutter)

Tarten hufen

Method

1. Mix the sugar and the gelatine, add to the double cream, then whisk the egg whites until the whites stand up in stiff peaks, and add them to the cream.
2. Put the raisins or the raspberries on to the pastry, and add the mixture. Cook it at a very low temperature for about 1 hour or until the tart has browned, and if at all possible then leave the oven door slightly open. The cream has a tendancy to boil and bubble over if you are not careful.

Ingredients

1 litre of double cream
2 egg whites
150gm of sugar
1 tablespoon of gelatine (flavourless)
Cup of raisins or fresh raspberries

Makes 2 small tarts or 1 large (I normally make 1 large in a square tin)

Ingredients for the Pastry

½ kg flour
100gm butter
50gm sugar
Warm water

Method

1. Mix the flour with the sugar and the butter, add warm water until you have a fairly smooth and soft dough.
2. Put it in the fridge for about ½ hour
3. Roll out and line your tin and fill with the mixture (see method above).

Conversion Charts

US measure	US volume	British	Metric
1 cup	8 fl oz	8.3 fl oz	237 ml
1 tablespoon	½ fl oz	0.52 fl oz	14.8 ml
1 teaspoon	1/6 fl oz	0.17 fl oz	4.9 ml

We have included a few ingredients for conversion
based on the recipes in this book.

Ingredient	1 cup
White flour	125 gm
Whole-wheat flour	120 gm
Strong white flour	140 gm
Rye flour	100 gm
Granulated sugar	200 gm
Brown sugar	220 gm
Icing sugar	120 gm
Long –grain rice	185 gm
Short grain rice	200 gm
Wild rice	160 gm
Cheese (hard) + grated	100 gm
Bacon (raw) + diced	225 gm
Fresh Breadcrumbs	50 gm
Cabbage (raw) sliced	100 gm
Butter/Fat/Lard/Shortening	225 gm
Carrots (raw) grated	50 gm